What Can You

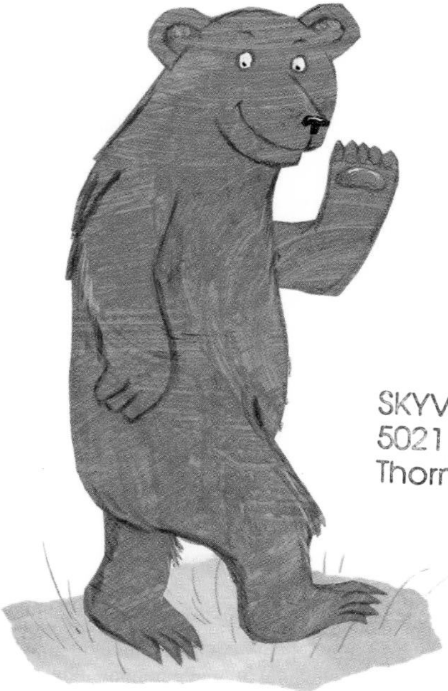

by Lada Kratky
illustrated by Cheryl Nathan

HAMPTON-BROWN

Spring

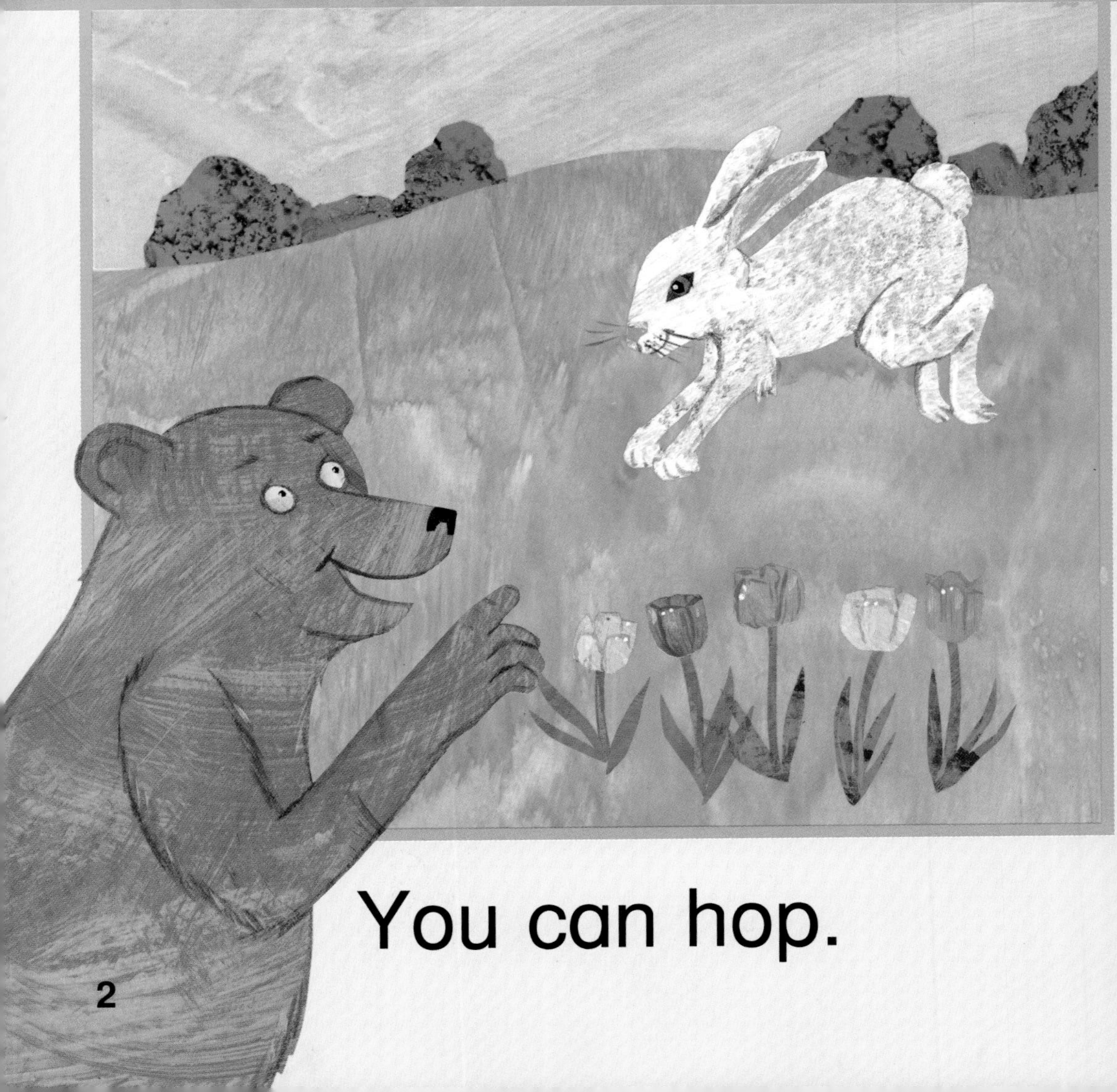

You can hop.

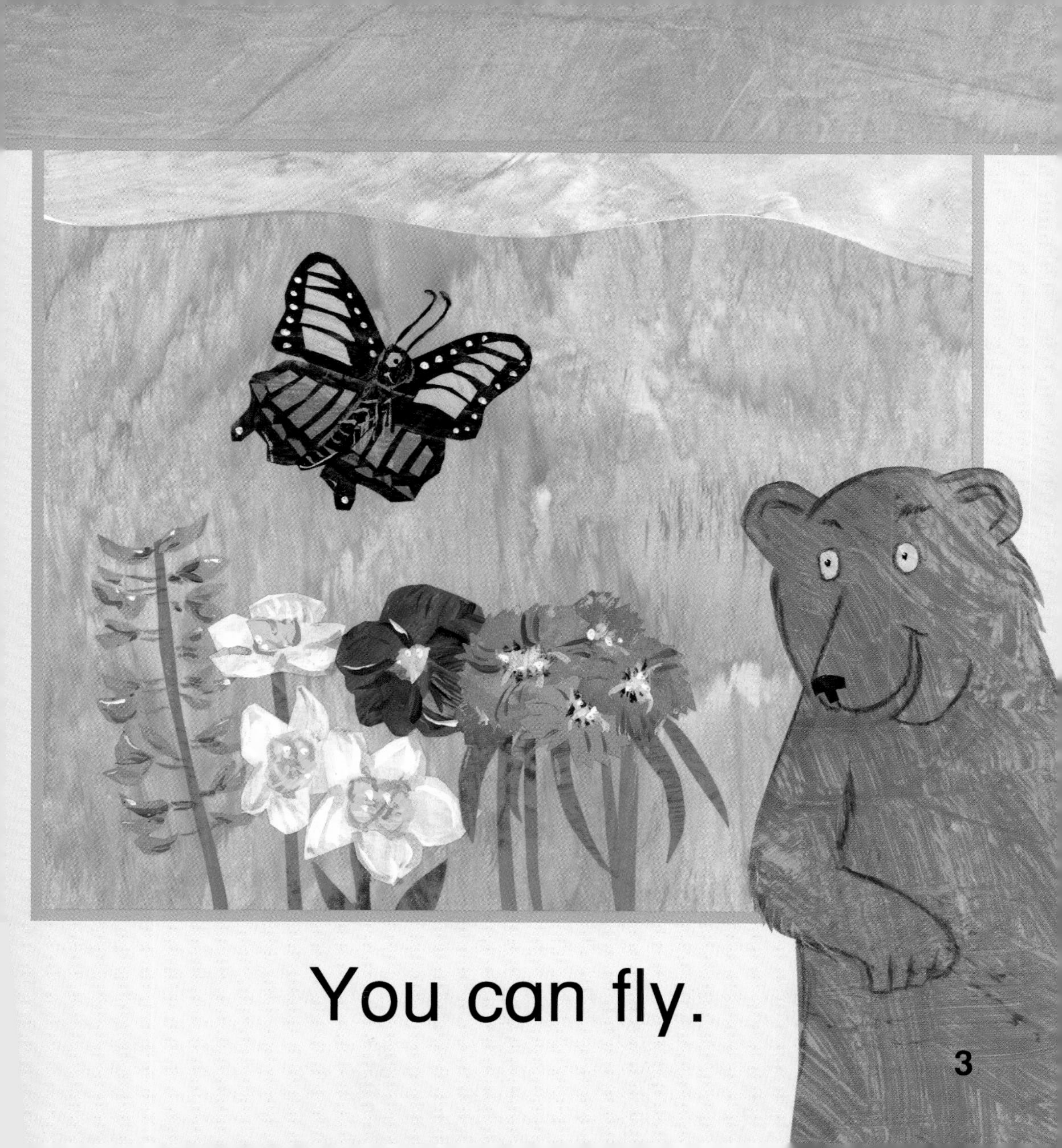

You can fly.

Summer

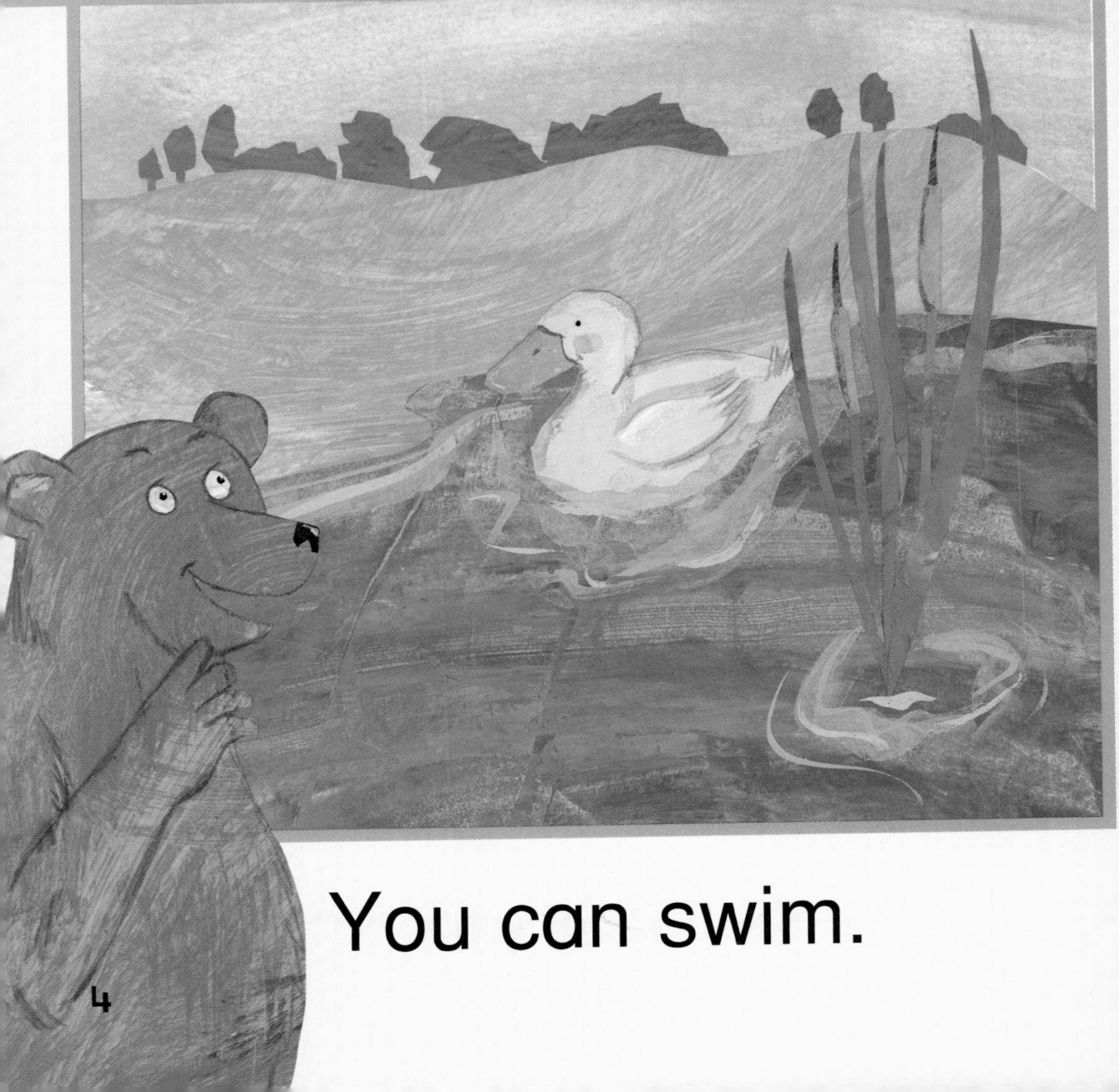

You can swim.

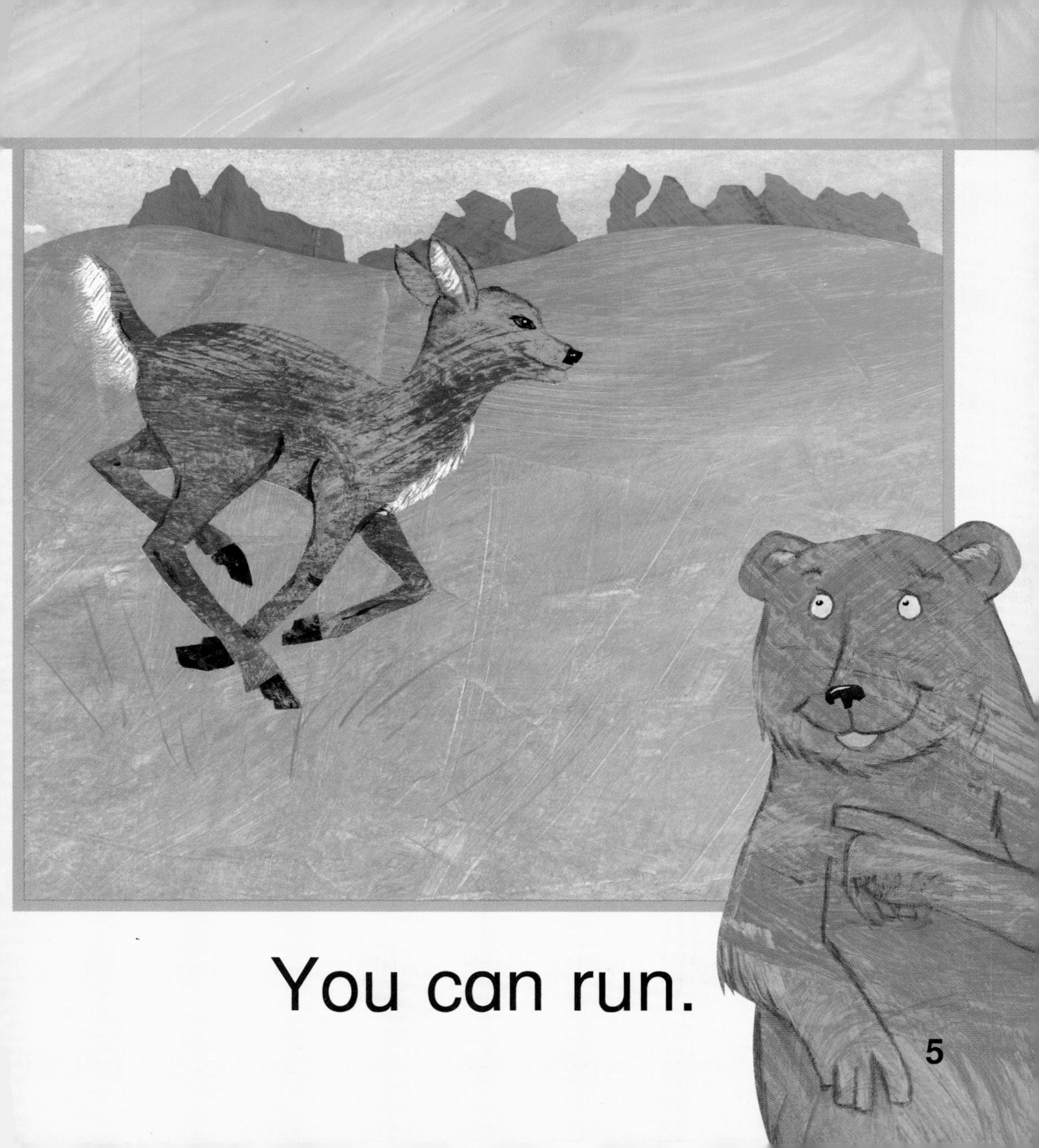

You can run.

Fall

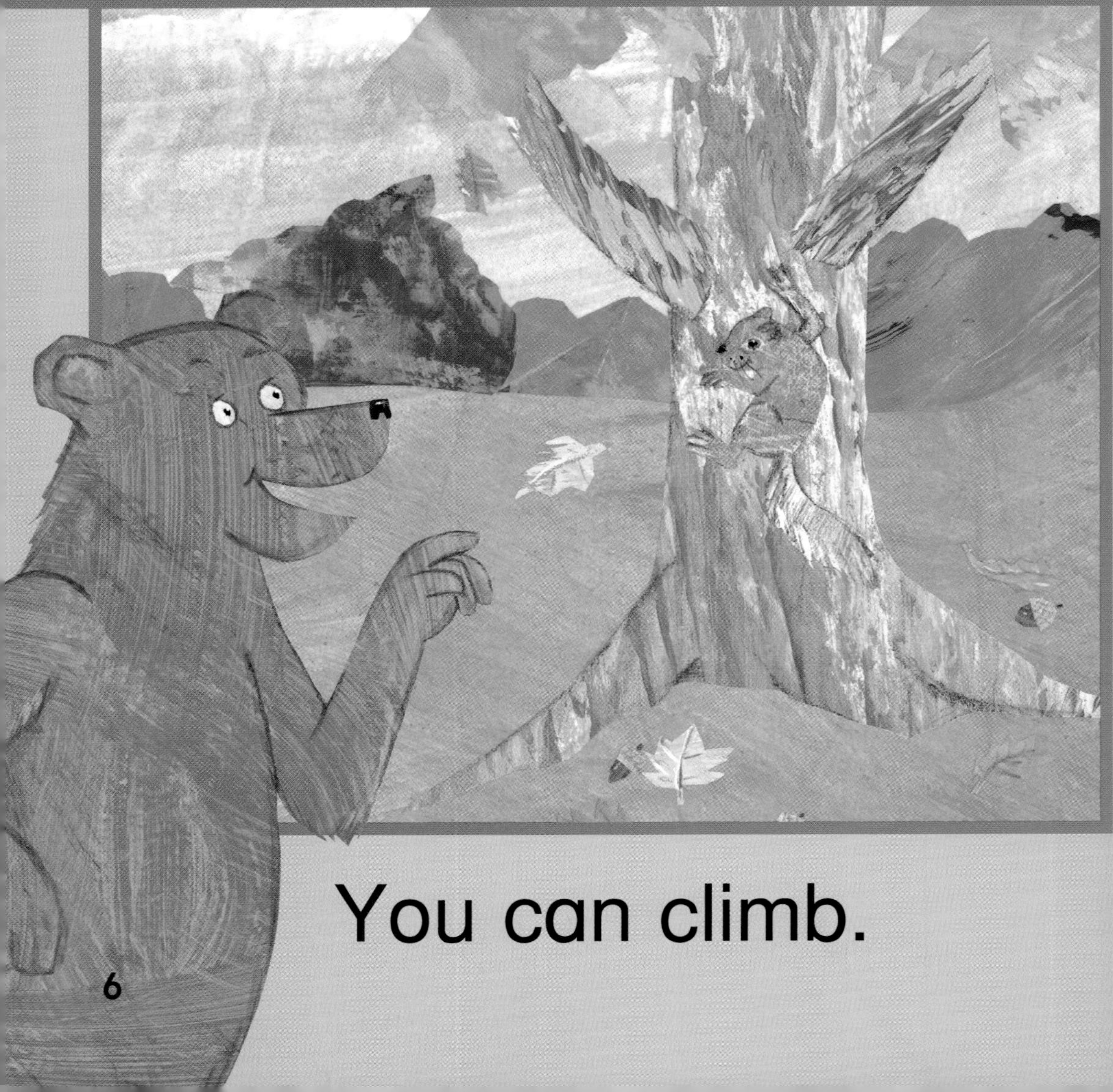

You can climb.

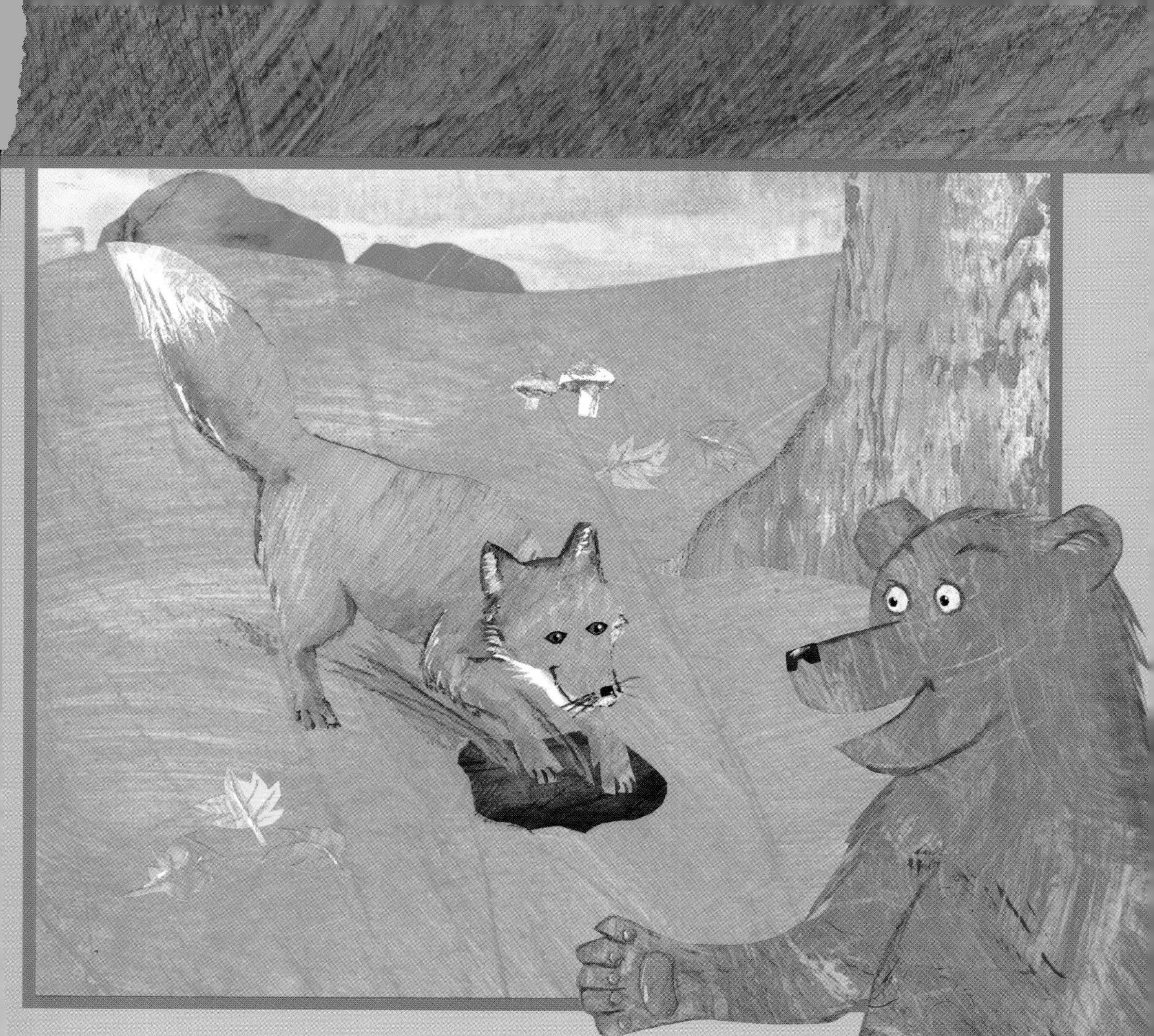

You can dig.

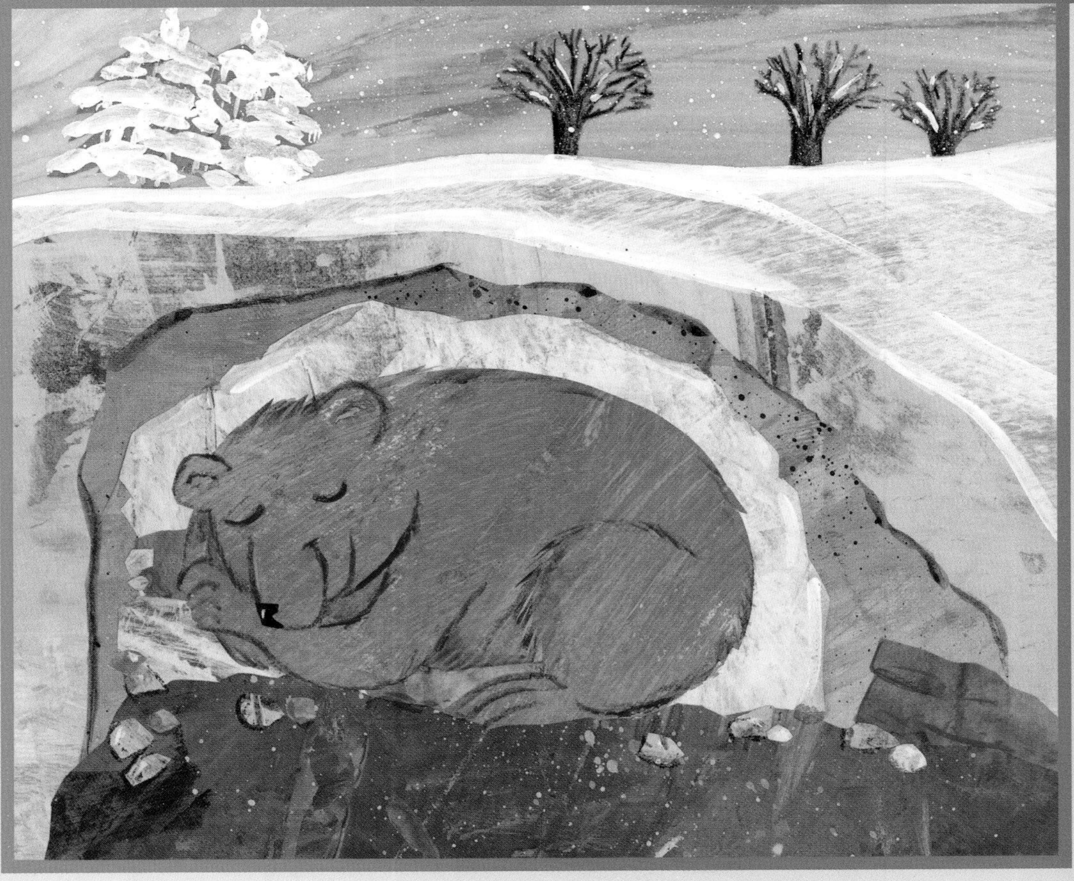

I can sleep.